you deserve flowers

you deserve flowers

(danny francis)

library partners press

ISBN 978-1-61846-116-2

Illustrations by Danny Francis
Cover art by Kristyn Larsen (Krislarsart@gmail.com)
Book and cover design by Celeste Holcomb

Produced and distributed by

Library Partners Press
ZSR Library
Wake Forest University
1834 Wake Forest Road
Winston-Salem, North Carolina 27106

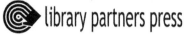 library partners press

a digital publishing imprint

www.librarypartnerspress.org

Manufactured in the United States of America

(about this collection)

i started writing poetry
for the same reason
i love planting flowers

(it makes me feel braver when i'm afraid).

i hope these poems
help you feel
braver too.
i hope they
are soft and fierce
and honest
in all the ways,
you need to hear.

(i hope they grow inside you and bloom in your hair like flowers).

some nights
i still dream
that i'm
sitting in the
waiting room,
shaking,
and heaving,
and staring at the floor
and desperately waiting
for you to show up
and tell me
the one thing i need to hear,
most in the world,
but can't seem to say
to myself,

(my dear,

this life is so messy
and fragile
and i know you're scared,
but,
there is nothing
in this world,
not a thing,
that could
ever
take away
even a
single

drop

of your
precious,
precious

worth).

breaking?

it's

all
just
the
hardest
part
of

growing

(said the flower to the seed).

sometimes

i still catch myself
looking for

you

in
grocery stores
and
coffee shops,

between
flower petals

and
the faces
of

strangers.

i wish i could curse you,
                    but that was never my kind of magic.

there is a necessary
grief

that comes
from

outgrowing

clothes
and
flowerpots

and old stories.

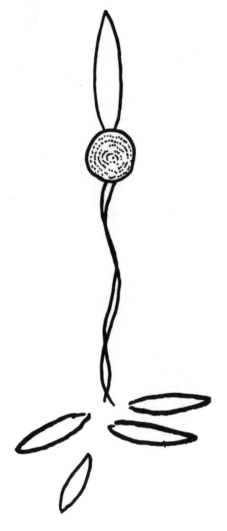

plant your softness

in your bare places.
bare as in naked,
naked like that
em-bare-rassing
scar on your
bare naked chin
from the first time
you cut yourself
shaving

or like the scar
from the first time
you fell in love.

and the second.

(plant there).

somedays

the metaphors
and
magic words
won't work

and life can't feel
like anything

except hard

(and that's okay, too)

talk about it
with crayons
and flowers.

it seems like really
tempting advice,
but *just be happy*
is not a substitute
for every painful,
messy, healing thing
you need to feel

right now.

take your time.

    sip your coffee
        slowly
        till you taste
        the honey
        at the bottom
        of the cup.
    be late.
        you can be late.
    spend time with
        all your needs
        (there are no small needs).
    rub the crusties
        from your eyes.
    brush your teeth.
    wash your hair.
    soak all your aches
    in the shower –
        your loneliness
        and lower back.
    be tender.
    take your time.
    take your time.
    put on your comfy clothes
        the one oversized shirt
        that makes you feel
        safe and small
        and held.
    fuck matching socks.
    feed the plants.
    water the dogs.
    water the plants.
    feed the dog.
    be distracted.
        you can be distracted.
    be soft.
        forgiving.
    set the heavy
        thoughts
        down as

gently as
you can.
tie your shoes.
(double knot).
left shoe
right.
take your time.
when you're
ready
and only
when you're
ready
open the door
and take that
first brave step
into the morning
sun.
then take another
and
another

and another.

morning grief
and
morning yoga

and

sipping coffee by the window
and
walking with a friend

and

grocery shopping
and
grilled chicken with peach salsa

and

maybe

just a little more
just a little more

acceptance

(and abs).

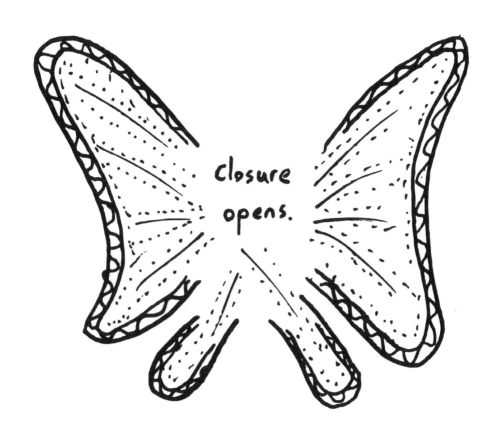

closure opens.

learn how to
hold these
words
in the

same

close,
gentle
way

you might
hold

    a shard of broken glass.

    a loose eyelash.

    a cicada shell.

    a newborn's chubby, pink
    fingers.

:

i am healing.

slowly.

bravely.
fiercely.

slowly.

i am healing.

it's so much harder to think about,

how she might be in love with someone else,

how many beers i have left in the fridge,

how unlovable i sometimes think i am,

when my friend makes a poop joke

in a crowded restaurant,

and we both start

laughing.

laundromats
and
longing
and
6:00 A:M runs
and
afternoon swims

and

lists
lists
lists
lists

and

compassion that grows
like the moon outside

my window

(and small steps).

it's not as easy
as they say,
falling in love
with your life

all at once,
all at once

(like they say you should).

but maybe
instead of
all at once,
you could

try spending
a few minutes
everyday

just loving,
just loving,

some of
your small
quiet details

(beginning with the shape of your toes).

tattoos
and
tangled hair
and
love handles

and healing traumas

and other things

that

don't make
you

less

loveable.

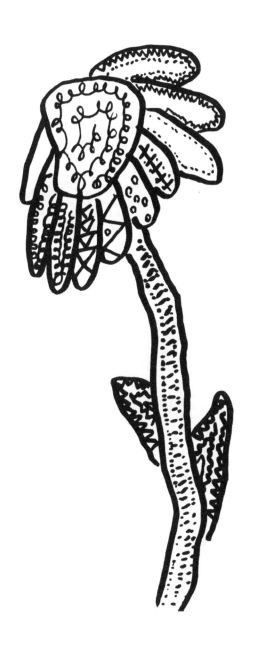

(remember)

you're not
blooming
for them.

every
morning

feed
yourself

sweet
words

sweet
strawberry
and
honey
words

that drip
from your mouth

and stick
to your

face

all day long.

you deserve flowers.

i once met a sunflower
with gold and crimson

hair.

i walked up to her
and shyly asked,

what's it like to bloom so softly?

without hesitation
she leaned in and
kissed my ear

and whispered,

i was just about to ask you the same.

be torn,
ripped, unevenly
down the middle,
like a sheet of paper
with dotted lines
you were supposed to cut,
but didn't.

(you beautiful failure).

be stained like glass,
like fragile, holy, colored glass,
like the place where the
fragile, holy, colored life
inside of you goes

to pray.

be a shapeshifter.
a dragon with lime-green polka dots
a pair of yellow stilettos.

a little braver.

be fearless
like a flower
with too many petals
spilling out

untamable colors,

reds,
and pinks,
and purples,
and oranges,
and greens,
and yellows,
and blues

in every direction

in every direction.

be like a poet

who only knows
one poem.

only one.

and
repeats it

over

and over,
and over,
and over,

and over

again:

you are

so wildly enough,
so wildly enough,

just as you are.

there are
parts of

you

that grow
better in the

sun.

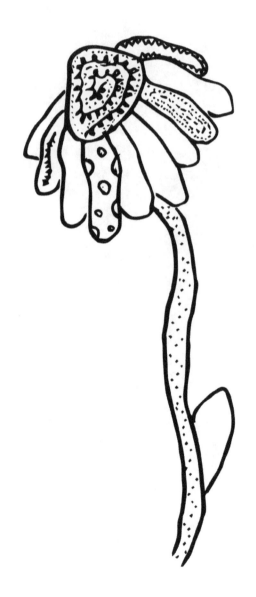

practice standing
in front of your mirror

(the one in your bathroom with toothpaste

    s   l

              p
                 a

                    t

                   t   e

                     r   d
                   e
                      all over it)

                      and

             telling yourself
               at least three

                   gentle,
                   naked,
                   loving

                   things

                everyday

           (until you can tell
                   yourself

                   four).

dear future lover,

would you
mind if
some nights
we could
try

just
holding,

just
holding

all of
each other's

doubts
and
longings

and

naked
insecurities

(and call that love making).

expressing needs.
asking questions.
holding boundaries.

(pillow talk).

tell me

about

all

the
sweet
healing things

growing in your heart

(please).

daffodils
and

self-trust
and

poppies
and

softness
and

marigolds
and

healthy intimacy
and

violets
and

just a little more boldness

(and other names for flowers).

and maybe,
and maybe,

you don't need to
punish yourself

for
every

flower

that
doesn't bloom.

your heart is not like
a department store diamond,
perfect and polished and gathering dust,
beneath layers of bullet-proof glass,
just waiting to be sold to the
right fairy-tale ending,
for the right price

($4,999.99,
plus, tax).

no.

your   heart is   more

like   a mud-covered-gem that you might find

while walking

barefoot and naked through a sandy,

mountain creek.

the kinda stone that's

jagged

and

u n e v   e

n .

the kind   you could spend your whole morning (or life)

turning
over

over

        and over

and over

      and over

         and over

             and over

                  and over

             and over

        and over

      and over

in your   hands,

             falling in   love with

    the   way the sun light catches

            each

      sharp, naked, gorgeous

        curve.

my dear,

i know that
there are still
somedays
you feel

so buried,
so buried,

in this dark place,

but i promise you,

the sun will rise
and the
rain
will come

then the work

and
you will
grow back,

with colors
that
bloom

like
laughter.

(the flower said me).

(Acknowledgments)

There are many people i would to thank for their support. i would first like to thank Library Partners Press for their continued support of my projects and my voice. i would especially like to acknowledge Jude Swanson for being a source of reflection and insight as well as a willing ear (even though he is not very good at foosball). i would like to thank Kristyn Larsen for her inspiring perspective and for creating the cover art for "you deserve flowers". If you would like to access more of her art, you can find her on Instagram @krislarsart. And finally, thank you to all those who loved my earliest scribblings on Instagram and who have watched my flowers

grow.

(about the author)

Danny is a recovery professional, farmer, theologian, and educator based in the mountains of Western North Carolina. When he is not writing poetry, or growing flowers in his beard, Danny is usually playing in the dirt, dazzling the world with his jokes, or driving around the mountains in his orange car.

This is his first book of poetry.

@theflowerbeardpoet

CPSIA information can be obtained
at www.ICGtesting.com
Printed in the USA
BVHW030835011120
592281BV00029B/443